FLUSH IT DOWN

THE STORY OF SEWERS THROUGH TIME

CONTENTS

EW GROSS!

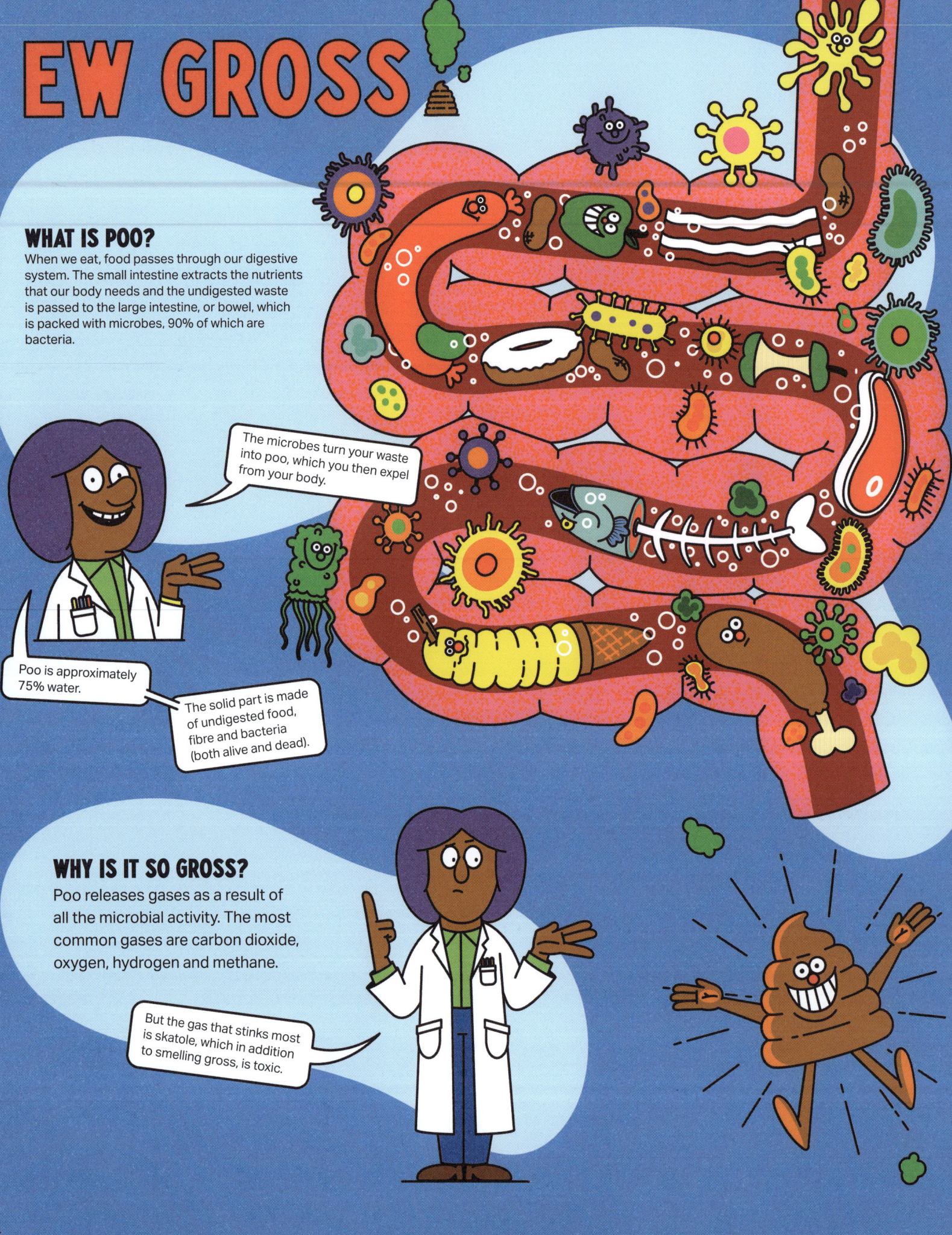

WHAT IS POO?

When we eat, food passes through our digestive system. The small intestine extracts the nutrients that our body needs and the undigested waste is passed to the large intestine, or bowel, which is packed with microbes, 90% of which are bacteria.

The microbes turn your waste into poo, which you then expel from your body.

Poo is approximately 75% water.

The solid part is made of undigested food, fibre and bacteria (both alive and dead).

WHY IS IT SO GROSS?

Poo releases gases as a result of all the microbial activity. The most common gases are carbon dioxide, oxygen, hydrogen and methane.

But the gas that stinks most is skatole, which in addition to smelling gross, is toxic.

Disgust is hardwired into the human brain.

Scientists have done studies that show that the part of our brain that processes emotion is triggered when we see or smell something disgusting.

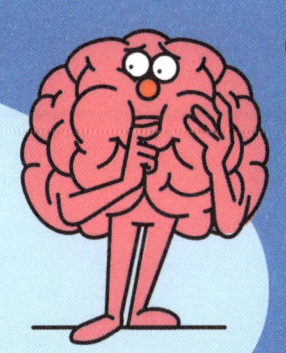
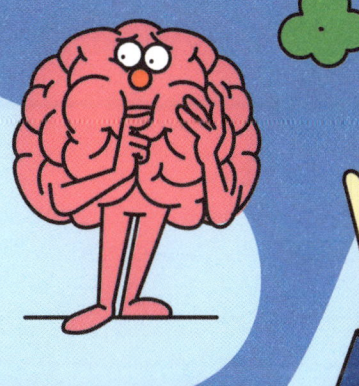

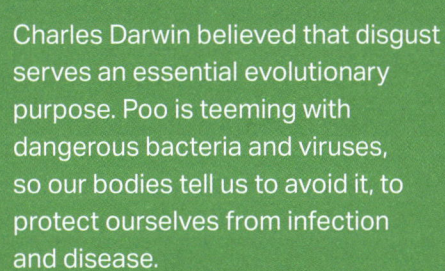

Charles Darwin believed that disgust serves an essential evolutionary purpose. Poo is teeming with dangerous bacteria and viruses, so our bodies tell us to avoid it, to protect ourselves from infection and disease.

CHARLES DARWIN

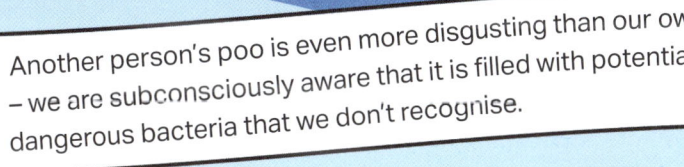

Another person's poo is even more disgusting than our own – we are subconsciously aware that it is filled with potentially dangerous bacteria that we don't recognise.

I ONLY WANT A HUG!

The physical response to disgust is universal. We wrinkle our noses and frown. Our blood pressure lowers and we often feel nauseous.

PREHISTORIC POO

Throughout history, people have found ways of keeping waste away from where they live. At first this was not a problem – people settled near rivers and springs and would poo in or near the water, which would wash it away.

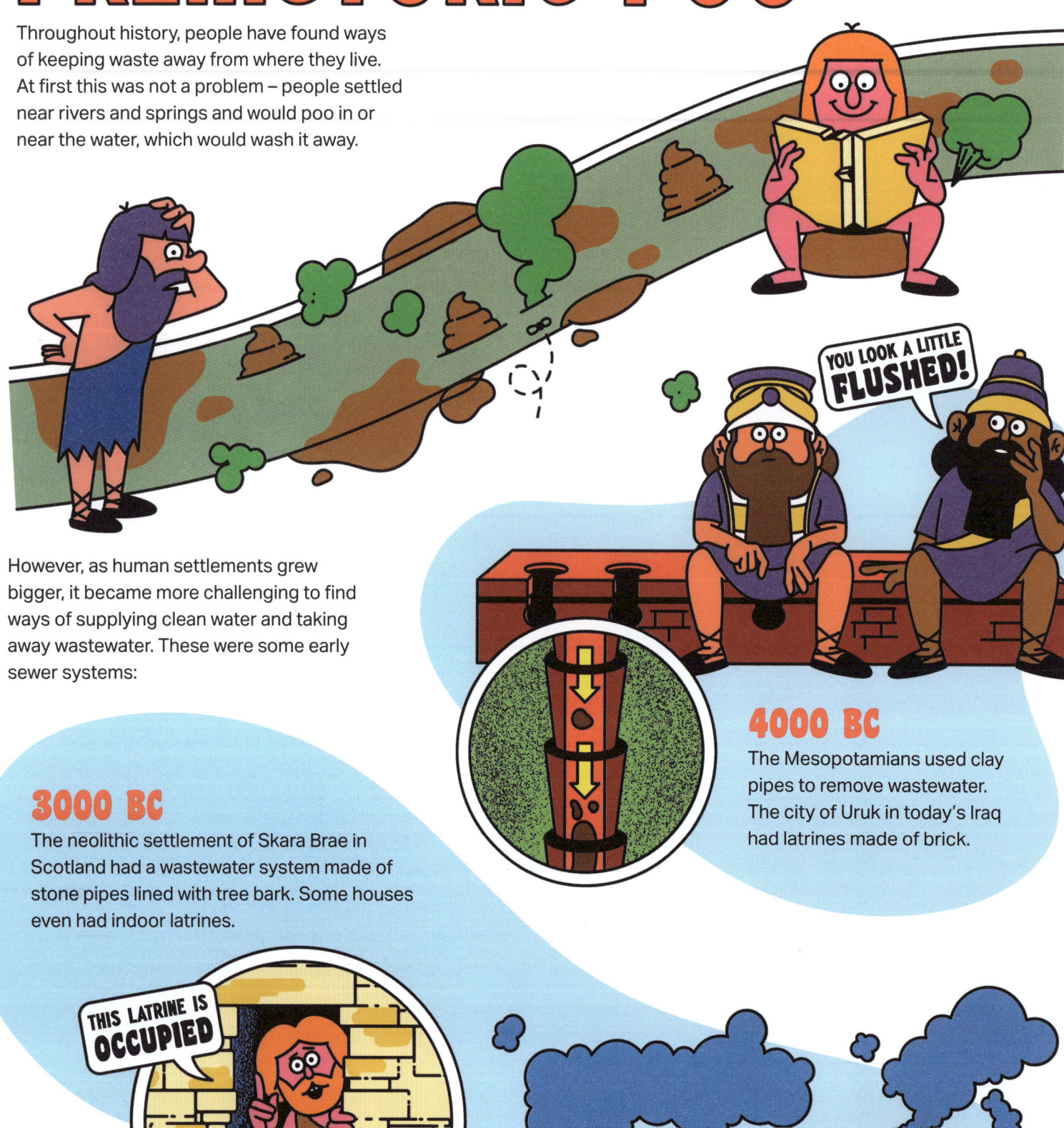

However, as human settlements grew bigger, it became more challenging to find ways of supplying clean water and taking away wastewater. These were some early sewer systems:

4000 BC

The Mesopotamians used clay pipes to remove wastewater. The city of Uruk in today's Iraq had latrines made of brick.

3000 BC

The neolithic settlement of Skara Brae in Scotland had a wastewater system made of stone pipes lined with tree bark. Some houses even had indoor latrines.

2500 BC

The city of Lothal in today's India had a sophisticated water system with brick drains leading from houses into large pits that were regularly cleaned out.

2000 BC

The Ancient Minoan civilisation in Greece had a complex clay pipe sewage system that connected toilets and sinks to a larger sewer, which had manholes and air shafts for ventilation.

CLOACA MAXIMA

600 BC - 300 BC

The Ancient Romans were the first to build a sewer system on a large scale. In the 6th century BC, a simple sewer was constructed to drain the marshlands in the centre of Rome and to carry stormwater down to the River Tiber, which ran beside the city. It was mostly made of open-air channels lined with brick.

CLOACA MAXIMA TRANSLATES AS **THE GREAT SEWER**

The Roman Forum, which was the central hub of the city, was built on top of the Cloaca Maxima.

As the city expanded, the waste problem became more serious, so the wealthy empire invested in a huge vaulted sewage tunnel – the Cloaca Maxima. This tunnel was 1600 m long and was so wide, a haycart could pass through it. The city was built on top of the sewer, with pipes connecting it to private homes and public baths.

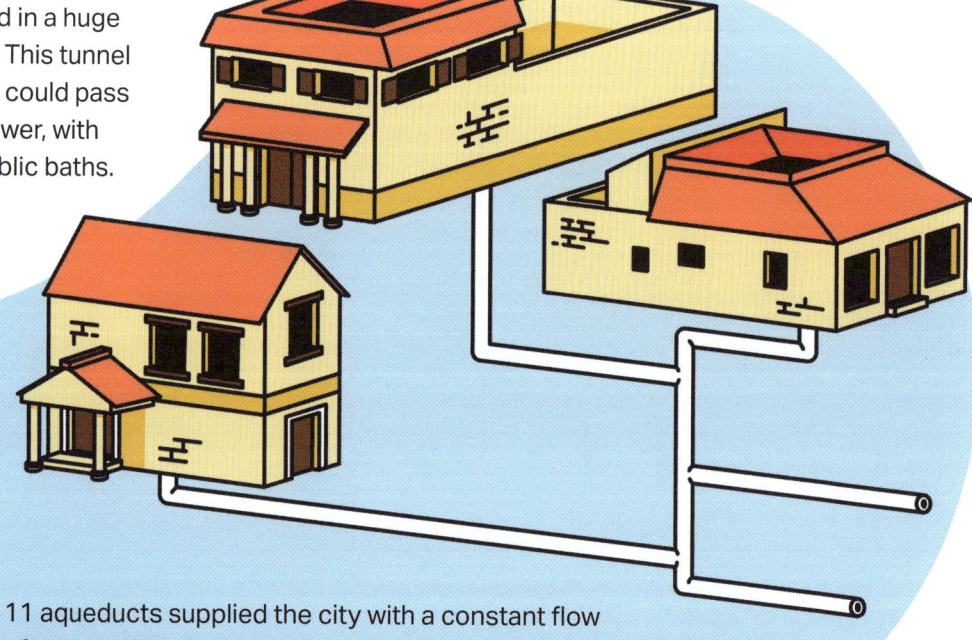

11 aqueducts supplied the city with a constant flow of water, which flushed the sewers and kept them free of obstructions. The Cloaca Maxima then drained the wastewater into the Tiber River.

9

EARLY MIDDLE AGES

476 - 1300AD

After the collapse of the Roman Empire, Europe split into smaller territories ruled by kings, generals, governors and warlords. Much of the knowledge and technology of the Romans was lost. In most medieval towns, there was no running water, no rubbish collection and no sewers.

The poor would place a stool with a hole in it over a basin to poo. They would then empty the basin into a nearby river, or often, just dump it out the window.

THAT'S WHY A POO IS CALLED A **STOOL!**

An open drain ran down the centre of the streets, carrying the waste to the nearest river. The city of York in the north of England had streets that were knee-deep in sewage.

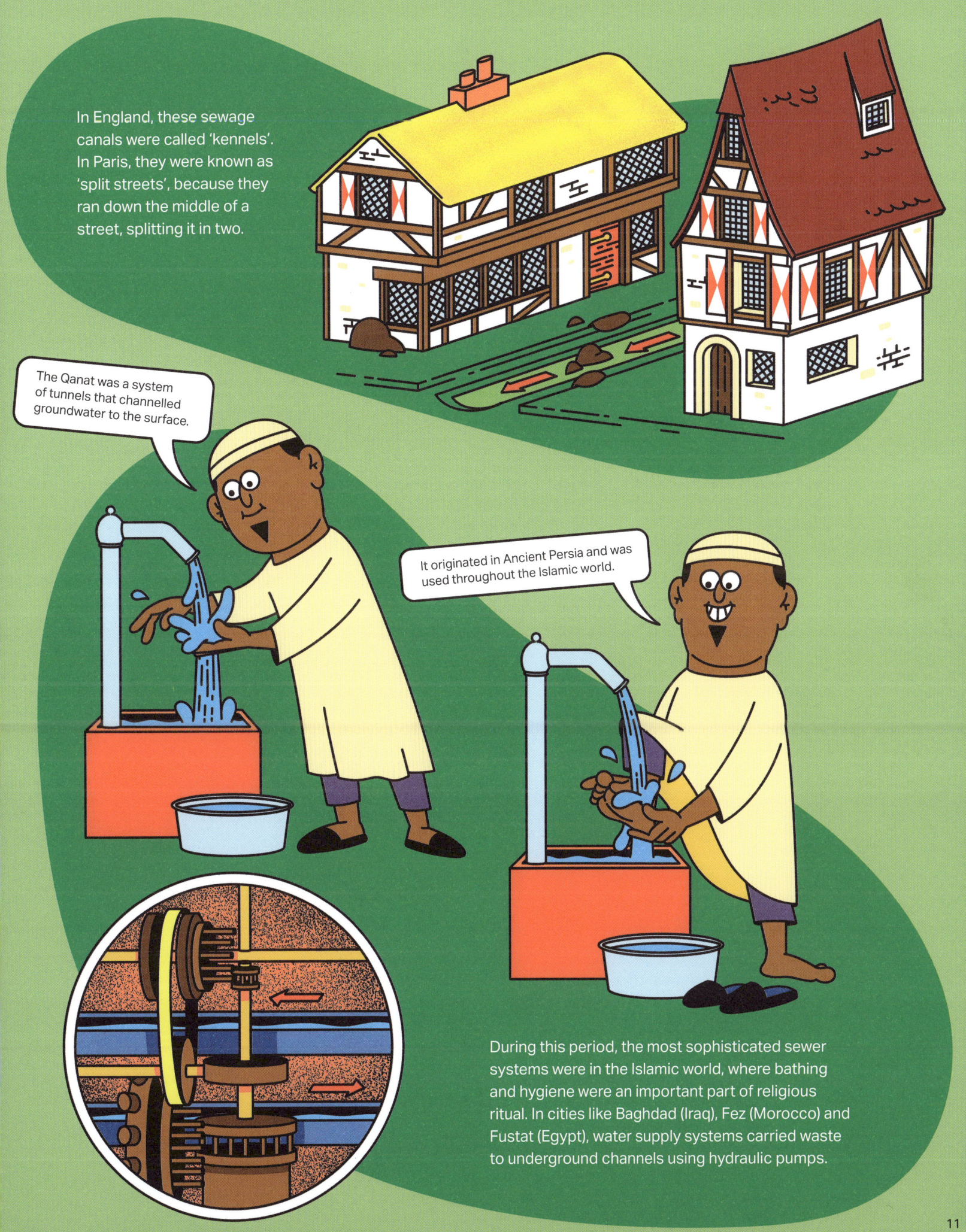

In England, these sewage canals were called 'kennels'. In Paris, they were known as 'split streets', because they ran down the middle of a street, splitting it in two.

The Qanat was a system of tunnels that channelled groundwater to the surface.

It originated in Ancient Persia and was used throughout the Islamic world.

During this period, the most sophisticated sewer systems were in the Islamic world, where bathing and hygiene were an important part of religious ritual. In cities like Baghdad (Iraq), Fez (Morocco) and Fustat (Egypt), water supply systems carried waste to underground channels using hydraulic pumps.

THE LOST ART OF
GONG FARMING
1400 - 1700 AD

As European cities grew bigger and more crowded, they also became dirtier. Public toilets, called latrines, were built… but not many. In the 1500s, London had only 16 public latrines for a population of about 40,000 people.

THE LARGEST PUBLIC LATRINE IN LONDON WAS AT LONDON BRIDGE.

WELL, SOMETHING'S FALLING DOWN, BUT IT'S NOT THE BRIDGE!

Wealthier people found their own solution by building cesspits under their homes. These pits were made of materials that allowed liquids to drain away, leaving the solid waste behind. Every few years, someone had to dig out the waste. This unpleasant and dangerous job was done by workers known as gong farmers.

Gong is an Old English word meaning 'to go'.

Gong farmers earned sixpence a day, which was considered good pay at the time.

However, the job wasn't respected by most people. Gong farmers were only allowed to work at night (they were often called 'night farmers'), and they were only allowed to live in certain places.

I WANT TO GONG HOME!

It also carried many risks. The cesspits they worked in were often poorly built and had no ventilation. In some cases, gong farmers drowned when parts of the cesspit collapsed.

There were strict rules about how the waste had to be disposed of. In London, it was taken to a wharf where it was loaded onto barges and carried away from the city.

In other places, the waste was spread on open land just outside the town, in areas known as sewage farms.

One gong farmer, who just dumped his stinking load, was punished by being buried up to his neck in a pipe filled with gong and put on public display.

BOOO!

BOOO!

BOOO!

Interestingly, human waste is rich in nitrate, and soil from the sewage farms was sometimes processed to make saltpeter, or potassium nitrate, which was a key ingredient in making gunpowder.

MY EXPLOSION CAUSED AN EXPLOSION!

SALT PETER

MEDIEVAL SEWERS

AROUND THE WORLD

While Europe was slow to solve its waste problems, other parts of the world were much more advanced in managing sanitation.

During China's Yuan Dynasty (1271–1368), the capital city of Dadu had an impressive citywide sewage system. The sewers were made from brick and covered with large stone slabs called flagstones. Some were built directly into the roads, while others were larger, domed tunnels that ran underneath the streets.

Between the 8th and 15th centuries, Spain was a wealthy and forward-thinking Muslim state called Al-Andalus. In the town of Murcia, archaeologists have discovered that, by the 11th century, most houses had their own toilets, which flushed waste into canals that carried it outside the city.

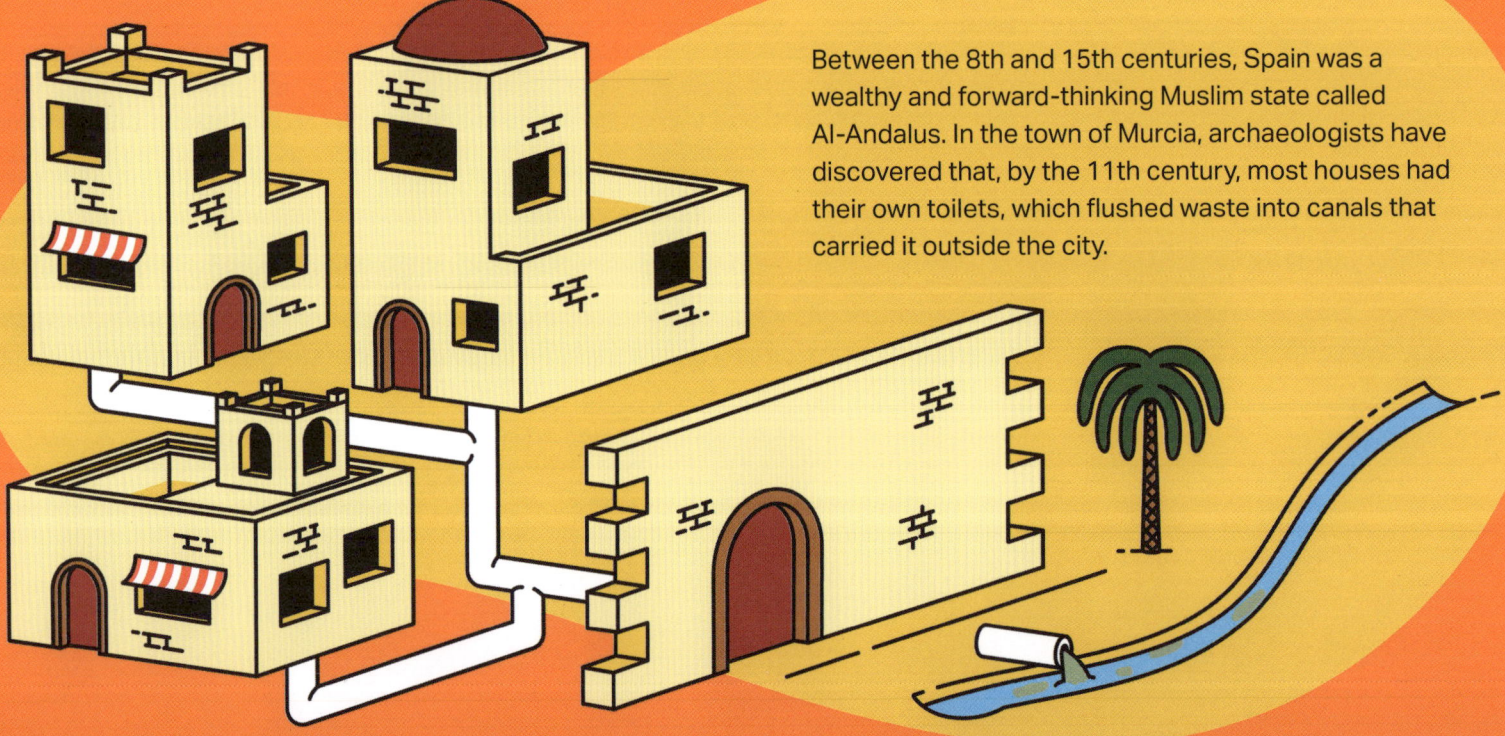

DISEASES
AND THE DIRTY CITIES OF EUROPE

DYSENTERY

Dysentery was one of the most deadly diseases. It spread through contact with poo-contaminated water or surfaces. It caused fever, vomiting and severe diarrhoea. Because people didn't know how to stop it from spreading, the disease could move quickly through communities.

In medieval Europe, cities were crowded and filthy, which made it easy for deadly diseases to spread. Waste from people and animals often got into the drinking water and the soil where vegetables were grown. Rats, mice and fleas were everywhere, carrying germs from place to place. These diseases were common during the Middle Ages and the Renaissance:

I'VE **BOTTOMED** OUT

BLACK DEATH

The Black Death, or bubonic plague, first arrived in Europe in 1346 and went on to kill nearly half the population. The disease was spread by fleas that lived on rats, which thrived in the dirty streets.

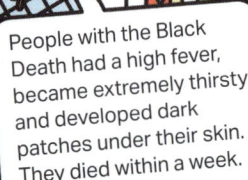

People with the Black Death had a high fever, became extremely thirsty and developed dark patches under their skin. They died within a week.

SMALLPOX

Smallpox was another dangerous illness. It was a virus that caused a high fever, sores in the mouth and a rash of painful blisters all over the body. Since it spread from person to person, it tore through crowded towns and cities very quickly.

TYPHOID

Typhoid was also common. It was caused by a type of bacteria found in food or water that had been contaminated with traces of poo. Because sewage often got into the drinking water, typhoid could spread rapidly.

Symptoms included fever, headaches, a rash, constipation and vomiting. Without treatment, typhoid could last for months and even be fatal.

Back then, people didn't know that germs caused disease. Instead, many believed that illness was a punishment from God for living a sinful life. The church was happy to encourage this view.

A **PLAGUE** UPON ALL YE SINNERS!!!

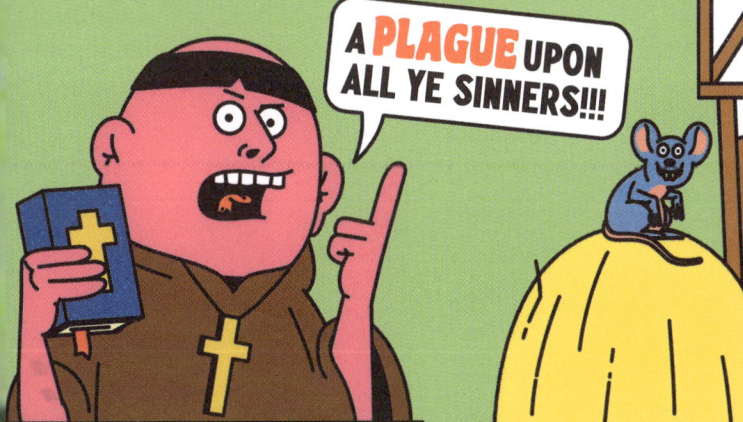

EVOLUTION OF THE
FLUSH TOILET

People have been using water to wash away waste for thousands of years, but the idea of a private flush toilet didn't come about until Tudor times.

NOW THAT'S WHAT I CALL A ROYAL FLUSH!

JOHN HARINGTON

SILENCE, JOHN! I AM SITTING ON THE THRONE!

1592

John Harington, the godson of Queen Elizabeth I, came up with a design that used water from an upstairs tank to flush waste into a cesspit below. However, his toilet needed 30 litres of water per flush. This was hard to manage without indoor plumbing, so the idea was put on hold for nearly 200 years.

1775

Alexander Cummings improved upon Harington's design. He added an S-shaped pipe (called a 'trap' or 'bend'), which allowed dirty water to flow out when flushed, but then sealed up again to block nasty smells from coming back in.

1851

A plumber called George Jennings invented the modern toilet. His design kept water in the bowl after the flush so the toilet stayed clean. Jennings showed off his invention at the Great Exhibition in Hyde Park, London – a huge fair showcasing the latest inventions from the Industrial Revolution.

GEORGE JENNINGS

Over 800,000 people paid a penny to try it out.

THIS LED TO THE POLITE PHRASE
TO SPEND A PENNY
MEANING TO USE THE TOILET.

1856

By the middle of the 1850s, the new 'water closet', or WC as it was referred to, had become popular and affordable, and featured in most middle-class homes across Britain and then America and Europe.

But there was a problem. With more people using flush toilets, a higher volume of waste was being dumped into cesspits and rivers. Big cities like London were overwhelmed, and things soon reached boiling point…

CHOLERA
AND THE 1854 BROAD STREET OUTBREAK

Cholera is a disease that still causes thousands of deaths today. Its symptoms are severe diarrhoea and vomiting. Without treatment, cholera kills about half of infected patients.

BROAD STREET

An untreated person with cholera can produce up to 20 litres of poo in a day.

Today, we know that cholera is caused by water that has been contaminated with human feces (poo) containing the Vibrio cholerae bacteria.

VIBRIO CHOLERAE

However, when it first appeared in Victorian times, it was believed that cholera was caused by miasma – polluted, smelly air.

EDWIN CHADWICK

A politician called Edwin Chadwick believed that by cleaning the streets of London, the smell would stop and cholera would disappear. He therefore insisted that all waste and sewage be washed off the streets and into the River Thames. Unfortunately, the Thames was the city's main source of drinking water, and soon there were more cholera outbreaks than ever.

On 31 August 1854, a massive outbreak in Soho, in central London, caused 500 deaths in just ten days. A doctor called John Snow suspected that the cause of cholera was drinking water, not miasma. He drew up a map that clearly showed that the deaths were concentrated around a water pump in Broad Street.

PUMP

I'M GETTIN' A HANDLE ON THIS NOW!

JOHN SNOW

Authorities removed the pump's handle and the deaths swiftly declined. Although Snow had proved that there was a link between dirty water and cholera, the government refused to accept his theory and replaced the Broad Street pump handle a few weeks later.

I FEEL GREAT!

BREWERY

A brewery on Broad Street was strangely unaffected by cholera. Snow discovered that this was because all the workers were drinking beer instead of water, and water is boiled before being used to make beer, thus killing off the bacteria.

THE GREAT STINK

During the Industrial Revolution, vast numbers of people left the countryside for factory jobs in rapidly growing cities. By the mid-1850s, London's population had reached 2.5 million. Flushing toilets emptied millions of litres of waste straight into the River Thames. While the city had numerous small sewers, they were poorly maintained and connected, failing to keep pace with the city's expansion.

The banks of the Thames were clogged with human waste, industrial runoff and animal remains from nearby slaughterhouses. In some places, the filth piled up over two metres high.

In the summer of 1858, London faced a serious crisis. It was unusually hot, with temperatures soaring to 36°C. The Thames' water level dropped and raw sewage was left sitting in the sun along the riverbanks, emitting unbearable smells.

THE EVENT WAS NICKNAMED
THE GREAT STINK!

At first, the government tried quick fixes, but the problem kept getting worse. The smell was so bad that even the British Parliament, which sat right next to the river, had to soak their windows in lime to try and block out the odour.

Finally, in 1859, the government took real action. They passed a law to build a proper sewage system for the city. A new group called the Metropolitan Board of Works (MBW) was created to manage the project and it was given a budget of three million pounds – a massive amount at the time.

SIR JOSEPH BAZALGETTE AND THE
GREAT LONDON
SEWER

The head of the Metropolitan Board of Works (MBW) was Sir Joseph Bazalgette, an engineering mastermind and visionary.

SIR JOSEPH BAZALGETTE

DON'T TELL ME IT'S JUST A PIPE DREAM!

He had spent several frustrating years drawing up designs for a radical new sewer system, only to see them cast aside whilst Parliament argued about cost. The Great Stink was the catalyst he had been waiting for. Finally, his plan was allowed to go ahead.

Bazalgette's solution was to build a massive sewer system under the streets of London that would divert the waste downstream to the Thames Estuary, far away from the city itself.

PUMP IT OUT

One of Bazalgette's greatest challenges was figuring out how to move sewage from the low-lying parts of the city – those below the high-water mark – into the main sewer system.

To address this, Bazalgette designed three pumping stations across the city, equipped with the largest steam engines of their time.

These stations lifted waste from the low-lying sewers to higher-level sewers, so that it could be drained away.

The biggest of these stations was at Crossness, on the eastern outskirts of the city. Four huge steam driven pumps pushed the sewage up by ten metres, pumping it into a giant reservoir, which then released the waste into the Thames as the tide went out, sucking it out to sea.

THE FOUR STEAM PUMPS WERE NAMED:

'VICTORIA'

'PRINCE CONSORT'

'ALBERT EDWARD'

& 'Alexandra'.

PRINCE CONSORT

SO CLEAN IT UP!

Joseph Bazalgette's new sewer system in London was a big improvement. But even after it was built, raw sewage was still being dumped into the River Thames, east of the city.

Then, in 1878, something terrible happened. A passenger boat called the Princess Alice collided with a coal barge – right where the city's untreated sewage flowed into the river. The water was so dirty and smelly that rescuing people was nearly impossible. Tragically, about 650 people died, either from drowning or from the toxic water.

A newspaper at the time described the situation like this: "Two continuous columns of decomposed, fermenting sewage, hissing like soda water with harmful gases, so black that the water is stained for miles and giving off a horrible smell that will be remembered by all."
— *The Times*, 6th September, 1878

After investigating the disaster, the government realised they needed to do more. Instead of letting sewage flow straight into the river, they began storing it in large tanks. Chemicals were added to separate the solid waste from the liquid. The liquid was still released into the river, but the solid waste, called sludge, was taken out to sea on special boats known as 'Bovril Boats' (Bovril was a thick, brown beef paste that was popular at the time).

POOP POOP!

SCIENTIST SAYS

Later on, scientists found that adding oxygen to the sludge helped reduce the terrible smell. This discovery was the start of the modern sewage treatment systems we still use today.

TREATMENT

TODAY

Modern sewage systems are designed to clean water safely, protect nature and even recycle waste into useful things. When you flush the toilet, or drain water from your sink, it travels through underground pipes to a sewage treatment plant. There, it goes through several steps to make it safe before it goes back into nature.

1 **GETTING RID OF BIG STUFF**
First, large items like plastic, wipes and other debris are removed using screens and grit chambers.

GREASE

SOLIDS

2 **SEPARATING SOLIDS AND LIQUIDS**
Next, the sewage sits in big tanks. Heavy waste, like poo and food scraps, sink to the bottom as sludge. Oily stuff floats to the top. Both are taken away. The liquid that remains is called effluent.

3 **CLEANING THE WATER WITH MICROBES**
Tiny living microbes and bacteria are added to the remaining liquid. They eat a lot of the contaminants, helping to clean the effluent.

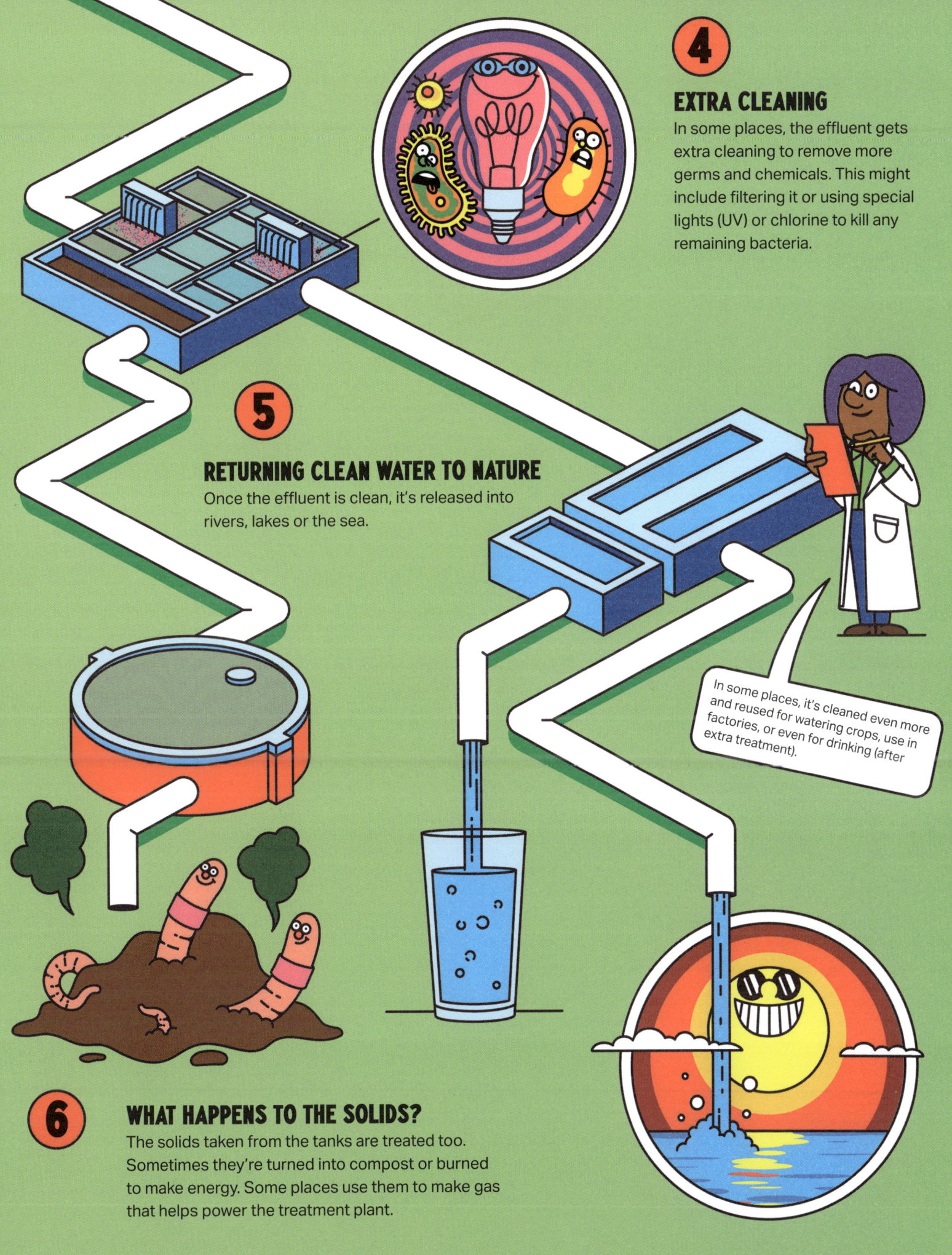

4

EXTRA CLEANING

In some places, the effluent gets extra cleaning to remove more germs and chemicals. This might include filtering it or using special lights (UV) or chlorine to kill any remaining bacteria.

5

RETURNING CLEAN WATER TO NATURE

Once the effluent is clean, it's released into rivers, lakes or the sea.

In some places, it's cleaned even more and reused for watering crops, use in factories, or even for drinking (after extra treatment).

6

WHAT HAPPENS TO THE SOLIDS?

The solids taken from the tanks are treated too. Sometimes they're turned into compost or burned to make energy. Some places use them to make gas that helps power the treatment plant.

Modern sewage systems are expensive and hard to build. Many poorer countries simply can't afford them.

In rich countries, about 74% of sewage is treated, but in developing countries, this number is only around 4.2%.

This means that untreated sewage often ends up in rivers, lakes and the sea. It harms fish, animals and the environment.

It can also leak into farmland, making crops unsafe to eat.

About one in three people around the world still don't have clean water to drink. Some use chlorine or special sand filters to clean water, but these methods are not reliable.

As a result, diseases like typhoid and cholera are still common in poorer parts of the world, even though they're rare in wealthier countries. As cities grow and more people need water, these problems will likely get worse.

There is hope, though. Natural solutions, like the building of wetlands, can sometimes offer simple, affordable ways of treating waste.

New technologies are also being developed. One example is the OMNI PROCESSOR.

This is a self-contained plant that takes in sewage and converts it into useful byproducts like clean water, heat and the electricity that the plant needs to power itself.

As cities grow and more people use the sewers, the pipes can't keep up. People also flush things like wet wipes and sanitary products down the toilet, which don't break down. These items mix with fat and oil to create huge blockages called fatbergs.

THE FUTURE OF SEWAGE

The future of sewage systems in the developed world is moving toward smarter, more sustainable and more energy-efficient solutions. Here's what's ahead:

LEAK DETECTED

SMART TECHNOLOGY

Sensors and AI will help monitor and control sewage systems in real time.

This will help detect blockages, leaks and pollution before they become serious problems.

LEAK

CITY

DRINKING WATER TREATMENT PLANT

This will help conserve valuable freshwater.

WATER RECYCLING

More cities will treat and reuse wastewater for things like irrigation, industrial use and even drinking.

SEWAGE TREATMENT PLANT

RIVER OR RESERVOIR

ADVANCED TREATMENT PLANT

ENERGY FROM WASTE

Modern treatment plants will increasingly generate energy from sewage sludge through microbial processes. Some treatment plants already produce more power than they use.

SMALLER, LOCAL SYSTEMS

Instead of massive central plants, there will be more small, local treatment units.

LOCAL PLANT

Especially in new neighbourhoods and housing projects.

This will save energy and cut connection costs.

SOLD

NUTRIENT RECOVERY

New technologies will extract useful materials (like phosphorus or nitrogen) from sewage to be reused in farming or industry.

CLIMATE RESILIENCE

Sewage systems will be redesigned to handle extreme weather.

They'll need to withstand heavy rains and droughts

so they don't overflow or break down.

Rain PROOF

DROUGHT PROOF

PUBLIC AWARENESS AND POLICY

People will become more aware of what goes down the drain and governments may tighten rules on what can be flushed or poured into sewers.

WHAT?!

GLOSSARY

AQUEDUCT

A special bridge or pipe that carries water from one place to another so people can have fresh water for drinking and for other uses. It has been in use since the days of Ancient Greece.

BAZALGETTE, JOSEPH

An engineer who built London's first big sewer system in the 1800s, helping to stop diseases and clean up the city.

CESSPIT

A hole in the ground where waste used to be collected before sewers were invented. People had to empty it regularly!

CHOLERA

A dangerous illness caused by drinking dirty water.

CLOACA MAXIMA

The great sewer that ran under Ancient Rome, allowing for sophisticated sanition throughout the city.

EFFLUENT

The liquid remains of sewage that has been treated in a septic tank or sewage treatment plant, and is therefore safe to be disposed of.

FATBERG

A huge lump of fat, oil and waste that blocks sewer pipes.

FLUSHING TOILET

A toilet that uses water to wash away waste. It became popular during the 1800s.

GONG FARMERS

People who cleaned out toilets and cesspits before there were proper sewers.

INDUSTRIAL REVOLUTION

A period of major technological advancement, particularly in manufacturing, that began in the late 1700s. It involved a shift from hand production to machine-based manufacturing, using steam and coal to power factories. It changed the way people lived and worked and caused a big influx of people from the countryside to the city.

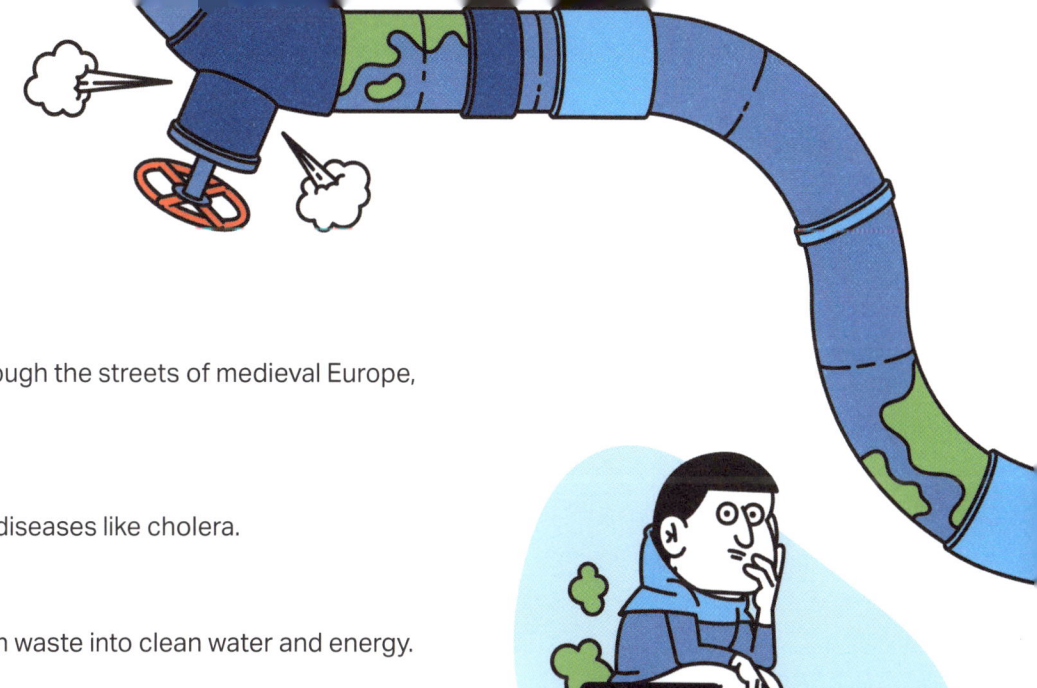

KENNELS
Open sewage channels that ran through the streets of medieval Europe, carrying waste to the river.

MIASMA
An old idea that bad smells caused diseases like cholera.

OMNI PROCESSOR
A modern machine that turns human waste into clean water and energy.

PUMPING STATION
A building with machines that help push sewage uphill into the main sewers.

QANAT
An ancient system of underground channels used to transport water from wells to the surface through a gently sloping tunnel. It originated in Ancient Persia and spread through the Islamic world in medieval times.

SANITATION
Keeping places clean to stop the spread of germs and disease – good sanitation means having proper toilets and clean water.

SEWAGE
Dirty water and waste that comes from toilets, sinks and drains.

SEWAGE TREATMENT
The process of removing contaminants from sewage to produce environmentally safe effluent and a solid waste that can be disposed of or reused.

SKATOLE
A smelly chemical that gives poo its bad smell.

SLUDGE
Thick, muddy stuff left over after sewage is cleaned.

WASTEWATER
Used water that comes from baths, kitchens, toilets and washing machines.

WATER CLOSET
An early name for a flushing toilet. The phrase WC is still sometimes used.

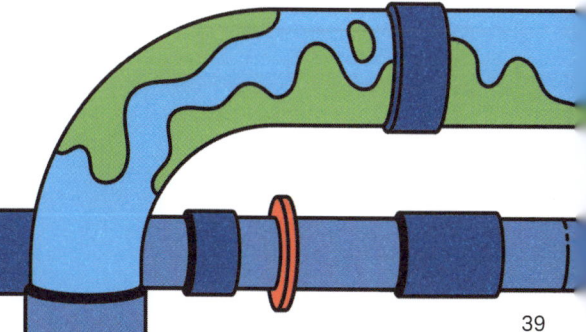

ABOUT THE AUTHOR

Born and bred Londoner Rob Flowers grew up close to where Bazalgette's Great Sewer released its waste into the River Thames. Rob is an illustrator with a distinctively bold style defined by crayon-bright palettes, playful forms and eccentric characters. His work draws on his fondness for mythology, combining whimsical imagery with symbolism and folkloric elements. Rob is the author of *Festival Folk* (Cicada, 2018) and the illustrator of *A Quick History of the Universe* and *A Quick History of Money* (Wide Eyed, 2020, 2021) and *Make Some Noise* (Puffin, 2024). Stationed in his 'Flowers Towers' studio, Rob is a keen collector of kitsch ephemera and historical miscellany, counting '80s gross-out toys, '70s cartoons and early McDonald's advertising memorabilia amongst his treasury.

FLUSH IT DOWN
Text by Rob Flowers and Robin Jacobs
Illustrations by Rob Flowers

British Library Cataloguing-in-Publication Data.

A CIP record for this book is available from the British Library
ISBN: 978-1-80066-064-9

First published in the UK in 2025, in the US in 2026.

Cicada Books Ltd
48 Burghley Road
London, NW5 1UE
United Kingdom
www.cicadabooks.co.uk

© Cicada Books Ltd, 2025

Printed in Poland on FSC certified paper